EMILIO'S VERY BRIGHT IDEA

Text copyright © 2022 by No Child Goes Hungry

Illustrations copyright © 2022 by No Child Goes Hungry

Library of Congress

Published by AK Classics

HARDCOVER

ISBN-13: 978-1-7378648-6-8

ISBN-10: 1-7378648-6-X

PAPERBACK

ISBN-13: 978-1-7378648-7-5

ISBN-10: 1-7378648-7-8

Printed in the Korea.

AK Classics

AK Classics
P.O. Box 77203
Charlotte, NC 28271
www.akclassicsstories.com

NO CHILD GOES HUNGRY.
NoChildGoesHungry.net

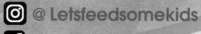

@ Letsfeedsomekids

@ Letsfeedsomekids

Emilio's Very Bright IDEA

Written by Louise Green
Illustrated by Penny Weber
Inspired by Kären Rasmussen

AUTHOR
LOUISE GREEN

Rev. Louise Green is an entrepreneur of the Spirit with various paths: congregational ministry, community organizing, and creative expression in writing, ritual, and movement. This is her first children's book, and she has a glimmer of an idea for the second.

Louise lives in Washington D.C. with her spouse and a menagerie of six animal companions. She resides near a wonderful community garden, with a good view of the playground at Truesdell Elementary School.

ILLUSTRATOR
PENNY WEBER

Penny Weber is a full time illustrator from Long Island, New York. She works on Photoshop creating digital paintings and has illustrated many picture books for the trade and educational markets. Penny lives with her husband, three children and their fat cat Tiger.

INSPIRED BY
KÄREN RASMUSSEN

Rev. Kären Rasmussen is the Founder and Director of No Child Goes Hungry, Inc. She is also an Affiliate Minister at the River Road Unitarian Universalist Congregation and at the Mount Vernon Unitarian Church.

Kären's social justice passion is to eliminate childhood hunger -- one meal and one child at a time. She has worked at several congregations in the DC Metro area organizing multigenerational social justice projects. Kären loves to garden and travel for recreation. She and her wife Barb, live in Annandale, Virginia with their rescue lab, Jemma.

Dedications

"We can do no great things.
Just small things with great love."

- Mother Teresa

The story of Emilio, based in my own D.C. neighborhood, is dedicated to every person and community working to make a difference. Each collective action for the good begins with a Very Bright Idea!

- Rev. Louise Green

To my thoughtful and generous of spirit wife Barb. You are as constant as the Northern Star and truly the wind beneath my wings.

For all the people and animals who have shaped what No Child Goes Hungry has grown to be, my heart is full of thanks and love for each and every one of you.

- Rev. Kären Rasmussen

Acknowledgements

Much appreciation to my sister, Kathy Izard, an author and teacher. When I pondered writing, she told me, "You can do this!" More thanks to colleague Kären Rasmussen, for her own Very Bright Idea, now No Child Goes Hungry. Her creative ministry inspires so many to take ideas into reality.

Every morning Emilio Antonio Santos De la O walked to school exactly the same way.

Now that he was in the 3rd grade, Emilio walked the four blocks alone.

He had his key on a straw sombrero chain from San Miguel de Allende, Mexico, where his grandmother lived.

He first walked along the big community garden and shouted,
"Hi there!" to Mr. Cleo Badgett, who was digging in the soft dirt.

Mr. Badgett had rows and rows of corn, climbing tomato plants, and baby squash growing on long vines.

Then Emilio counted the thirteen
peach trees in the garden and saw how
the hard green fruit was ripening.

"Good morning, peach trees!"

Next, he walked over to see the house with his favorite little dog, Whopper, and the Buddha statue in front.

"Hello Buddha! Hello Whopper!"

Finally, Emilio landed in the school playground and went up the climbing tower.

He sat high on top and watched all the people come into school like birds, flying into a very big nest.

After looking for a long time, Emilio climbed down and went into his school, Truesdell Elementary, just before the bell rang.

His first class that morning was his favorite – social studies!
His teacher, Mr. James Dixon, began showing lots of slides with children's faces and numbers.

He explained how all around the city of Washington, D.C.,
all over the U.S.A., and the world, kids were too hungry.

Even at Truesdell Elementary School, too many kids were hungry. Emilio's face began to scrunch as he thought about it. He knew some students ate breakfast in the cafeteria before school started, and also got lunches with vouchers.

Then a memory of his grandmother, Abuelita Corazón, popped into his head. He loved to visit her in Mexico in the summer with his parents, and always asked for the same birthday dish.

Emilio loved mole enchiladas, dark spicy chili sauce with grated chocolate, poured over hot hand-made corn tortillas with melty cheese. When Abuelita put that steaming plate on the table, she always shouted the same words and gave Emilio a big hug.

"La comida es amor, m'ijo!
La comida es amor!"

In social studies class, Emilio's arm started to wave in the air like the flag on the school pole in high wind. Mr. Dixon sighed and asked.

"Emilio, what is so important that you have to say it right away?!"

Emilio took a deep breath and thought about all the hungry children in the pictures. Abuelita's voice was singing in his head, so he yelled out very fast,

"La comida es amor!"

The class giggled and wiggled in their seats.

Mr. Dixon stared at Emilio and asked, "Excuse me? What does that mean?"

Emilio repeated more slowly. "La comida es amor," Abuelita always says. "It means, food is love. Mr. Dixon, hungry kids here at Truesdell need to eat because they need love. We have to DO something!" There was silence in the room, and now everyone stared at Emilio.

Mr. Dixon sat down on the edge of his desk and put down the remote control.

Then he spoke slowly, "What do you think we need to do, Emilio?"

Emilio Antonio Santos De la O thought very hard and wasn't sure what to say. He wished his arm had never flown up in the air like the flag on the school pole.

Then a tiny idea suddenly came to Emilio, like a little light bulb popping on. "What if hungry kids could go to a pantry at the front of our school and just take something home to eat?" Emilio spoke faster now, as his idea grew even brighter.

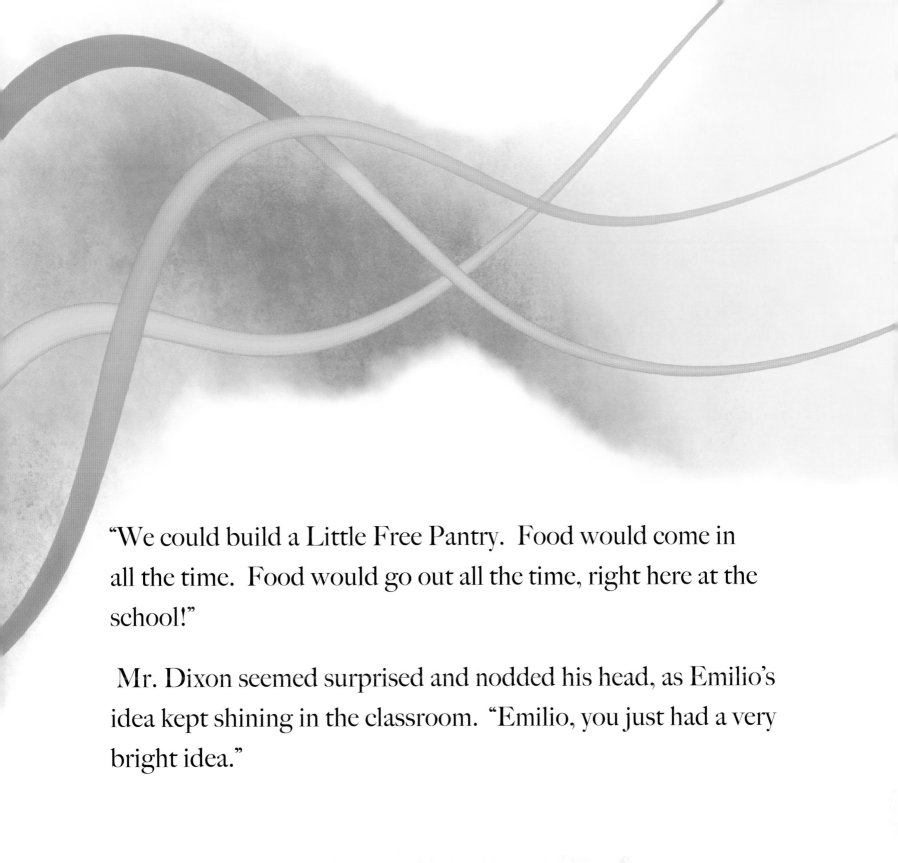

"We could build a Little Free Pantry. Food would come in all the time. Food would go out all the time, right here at the school!"

Mr. Dixon seemed surprised and nodded his head, as Emilio's idea kept shining in the classroom. "Emilio, you just had a very bright idea."

At lunch, Emilio's friends ran to catch up, wanting to talk about the very bright idea. Sunya Parikh, Eddie Cruz, and Omari Jackson were also excited because it was Friday, their favorite lunch day... pizza!

They each said what they would bring to the pantry for hungry kids. Omari said she would bring peanuts. She liked the thick sweet peanut and kale stew her Auntie Flo made in South Carolina. Sunya was going to bring in chickpeas. She loved to cook chana masala with her older brother and pour the spicy tomato sauce over basmati rice.

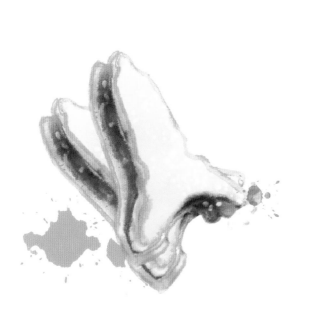

Eddie Cruz would contribute peanut butter and strawberry jelly. His mom was an architect and made sandwiches in little tower shapes with cookie cutters.

Emilio knew exactly what he would bring: dark unsweetened chocolate for mole sauce, the kind in Abuelita's kitchen.

When he left school that day, Emilio passed the front steps, and
imagined a new wooden cabinet of food sitting right there.
He could see it now: a Little Free Pantry to hold food for hungry kids!

It took a while for the Little Free Pantry to be built. First, Emilio needed to explain his very bright idea to even more grown-ups. Then money had to be raised and supplies purchased. People worked together to cut wood, build the cabinet, and paint the pantry in bright colors.

Finally, it was all done.

Emilio and his parents put the first food in the Little Free Pantry.

They opened the shiny purple and green doors that smelled like wood and fresh paint.

They put rice, beans, tortillas, chili powder, and dark chocolate inside. Emilio's very bright idea was real!

Truesdell Elementary School had a big potluck dinner to celebrate. There was chana masala and basmati rice, peanut and kale stew, peanut butter jelly banana towers, and enchiladas with mole sauce.

There were Friday cheese pizzas, too! Mr. James Dixon brought little packages of Oreos, and there were fresh pies from the peaches in the community garden.

At the very end of the first ever Annual Truesdell Picnic Fiesta, there was a special speaker.

Abuelita Corazón flew in from Mexico to celebrate the Little Free Pantry.

She stood up on a milk crate and shouted in a very excited voice, "Don't forget, m'ijos!

La comida es amor!

Food
is love.

Let's feed some kids!

Would you like to make a difference in your community like Emilio did?

Check out the No Child Goes Hungry website at www.NoChildGoesHungry.net for ideas. You'll also find free downloadable lesson plans for all ages that you can easily tailor to your needs.